A Poem is a Parachute

Megan Schaffner

A Poem is a Parachute

Thanks and Acknowledgements

Many thanks to the editors of the following anthologies and journals
in which some of these poems have appeared:
A Net of Hands: an anthology of Tasmanian Poetry, FAW Tasmania, 2009;
Of Things Being Various, 40 Degrees South, 2011 (from the manuscript
that won the national FAW Community Writers' Award in 2010);
Island Magazine; *The Green Fuse*, ed. Carmel Williams (Picaro Poetry
Prize Byron Bay Festival, 2010); *Blue Giraffe* and Republic Readings.
'Dancing with David Hobson' won the Hobart Poetry Pot in 2010.

Special thanks to my friend and poet supreme, Gina Mercer, who
has helped and encouraged me to put this poetry collection together.
And to all my writing friends, in poetry, fiction and memoir
writing groups – particularly to Karen Knight, Liz McQuilkin, Liz
Winfield and Christiane Conesa-Bostock, and to Avril Caney, Wal
and Berenice Eastman and Annette Sumner – I have thrived in the
warmth of your friendship and wisdom; I salute and thank you all.

A Poem is a Parachute
ISBN 978 1 74027 939 0
Copyright © text Megan Schaffner 2015
Cover image: Giles Hugo

First published in this form 2015
Reprinted 2016

GINNINDERRA PRESS
PO Box 3461 Port Adelaide SA 5015
www.ginninderrapress.com.au

Contents

The undiscover'd country	9
A Poem is a Parachute	10
Revenant	11
Mother Tongue	12
Sardine Run, Natal South Coast	16
Shadow Rising	18
Not-quite-everyone is singing	19
Black on White	21
Passionfruit	22
Of things being various	23
Words Fall as Rain	24
Dancing with David Hobson	26
suddenly spring…	27
Your skin to my touch…	28
Talk	30
On Peron Dunes	31
Siren Song	32
saltwater dreams	33
Adrift in the Desert	34
Cook	35
Purnululu Pilgrimage	36
Ruined Piano Sanctuary	37
Assisi	40
Leaving Beijing – Terminal 3	44
Digging	45
Grandmother Annie	47
Poem Rising	49
Wool Gathering	51
Lucy Turns the World	52
Boy on the Trampoline	53

For the tear is an intellectual thing	54
Wybelena Moonbirds	55
She-oak at First light	56
Old Men and Birds	57
From the far country of grief they come…	58
Raymond	59
Letter to Peggy	60
Woman in the Jade Felt Hat	61
When you phoned last night…	62
Letter to Jean	63
The tempest in my mind	64
The Unravelling	68
Onions and Aftershave	69
Coffee at the Signal Station Café	70
Every Day a Blue Door	72
Every Twenty-two Minutes	73
The Wasteland – Ninety Years on	74
Flying West	75
Artists Retreat from Jeanneret Beach	77
Pointed Bone	78
The Galaxies of Jackson Pollock	79
Dancing with the Sun	80

In memory

of Denis Graeme Schaffner,

who enriched my life immeasurably

1922–2013

The undiscover'd country

The world outside my window
is beautiful beyond belief,
slow blue hills lie gently
on the pale water,
a sail and its reflection
burn like a white flame,
a glinting knife
and below the window
rain-washed eucalypts.

Stand beside me friends
who have gone into the light,
this is my world,
see what I see –
and bring me word of yours.

A Poem is a Parachute

Jump!
Head in the clouds
it holds you
opens out
billows into silken images
delights you with expansive meanings
floats you gently to somewhere you've never been before
with luck
you'll land wrong side up
exhilarated
ready to explore a new country.

Revenant

Suspended between continents,
between birthplace and destination,
her body begins the slow
metamorphosis
to wandering albatross.

Bones elongate,
        hollow,
flesh thins to parchment,
words elide to a long harsh cry
as she flies above endless cloud tundra
through roofless halls of air.

Beneath the dark sun
sleeping on the wing
she is one with countless souls
for whom home is an unknown
word in a foreign tongue.

Mother Tongue

After years of constant sunshine
clouds tower overhead.
The children hear in wonder
water thrumming on the roof
and gurgling into tanks.

Gleeful
under gushing downpipes,
faces skyward,
mouths agape,
they taste
and tongue a new word
rain.

Splashing in the backyard
they build two towers of kero tins –
London Bridge –
they know it from their picture books.
A crowbar spans the muddy Thames.
After dark their father
stumbles
searching for the cat.
London Bridge is falling down…
Now the air's electric
with new words.

*

They wake
to see the world transformed
with colours from their crayon box –
a once-in-seven-years spring.
Sunny days
spent watching beetles, bees,
sniffing honey,
wading among flowers,
orange, yellow, white,
scrubby bushes bright with buds,
succulents of jewel colours.
Their mother names them and they sing:
Daisy   Gazania
Mesem-bry-anth-emum.
Misa-ribble–anthems,
laughs their father
as he piggy-backs them home.

*

Night on the Karoo,
a heavy frost of stars.
They stand outside
clutching their father's hands,
cold nibbling their toes.
Stones throw black shadows.
Listen, says the girl
in the hissing silence,
Listen to the stars.

Mkwena says the stars
hunt with their dogs
across the sky at night.
Tssik and Tsaa they say…
The brown dog whines,
quivers in the starlight.

*

Next day
with stones and circles in the sand
their father shows them planets
wheeling round the sun.
The world expands,
words explode around them.
She holds the sun-stone to her cheek
its coolness startling in the heat.

*

Red globes glisten,
rough stems and leaves
rasp against legs and knees.
In the irrigation ditch
mud oozes coolly
between their toes.
They pull the bursting fruit
'Mato, tomato
and bite, suck, slurp
the lusciousness.
Small yellow seeds stick to their cheeks,
dripping juice stings scratches.

Glut, they mimic, *Glut*,
hearing the farmer
speaking to their mother.
The girl picks off a small green star,
crushes the bruised redness in her mouth.

*

Winter
bare stony ground,
a cold wind blows dust
across the barren plain.

Their mother's ill.

Nameless shadows fill the house,
lowered voices, half-heard conversations
about *new monia*.
Strangers come and go,
shake their father's hand.

Night journey on the train
to stay with distant relatives
who never mention her
but give them coloured sweets
that taste of pain –
Cat's got your tongue –
they gently tease.

Bewilderment,
a glut of grief –
there are no words to tell
the sharpness
or the weight of stones.

Sardine Run, Natal South Coast

3 September 1939

Sardines are running up the coast...
See you on the beach at dawn.

Sleep-tousled children run
behind striding fathers, stumble
on dead eels and parrot fish
discarded by night fishermen.
Look – out there! Patches of grey
boil beyond the breakers,
gulls scream and dive.

In dank urine-smelling sand
the children dig a submarine,
they shoot the thieving gulls
with bamboo guns.

Lines skreel and arc, barbed lures
torpedo the farthest waves, lines tauten,
dripping light. A snap and drawn out skirl,
rods bend as flapping shad are dragged
in dozens from the rising tide.
                       The sea lightens.
On a long cast a fisherman hooks
the sun over the horizon.

That afternoon the children watch
solemn adults round the dome-topped wireless,
hear strange words of war.

Weeks later all their fathers left
in kilted khaki splendour
for whispered destinations –
talk of troopships and torpedoes,
and bodies washed ashore…

See you on the beach at dawn.

Shadow Rising

Standing in the kitchen,
secure in four-year-old self-confidence,
I pick up Samson,
the white cat who's adopted us,
push him on the glowing stove.

My mother enters
as he flies off, yowling.
She gathers him, comforts him,
tends his burnt paws.

Why? Why? she asks.
I cannot speak, stunned
by what I've done.
He trusted you…
She turns away
with Samson in her arms.

The stink of burning fills the house.

Something shifts beneath my feet.
Now nothing is secure.
For good or ill,
I have the power to choose.

My world is flawed
and through the rift
I glimpse the crawling dark.
A shadow rises,
stands beside me.

It will not go away.

Not-quite-everyone is singing

Shrill penny whistle
cheeky in the heat
piercing the siesta of a yellow afternoon.
Thud of the bass
from a rusty oil drum
and the taut-strung wire
of a backyard bow.
Dusty feet
beating out a rhythm,
lithe young bodies
dancing intricate patterns,
leaping from the shadows –
deep purple shadows
that lie along the pavement
under manicured trees.

> *A-ma-LE-le, ku-LE-le,*
> *Everyone is singing!*

Raucous ululations
of the servant women watching,
cocking a snook at the slumbering suburb,
drawn to the back gates,
supple hips swaying
to the *kwela* beat –

> *A-ma-LE-le, ku-LE-le –*

And the penny whistle player
capers, tumbles to the laughter –

> *Jonas! Tell those boys to stop that noise!*
> *Don't they know that people are resting after lunch!*
>
> *And tell Selina the work is waiting for her in the kitchen!*

Words fly derisively in fast syncopation,
rise above the rooftops
like flocks of startled hadedas.
The women scatter with insolent swaggers,
shut backyard gates with provocative clicks.

The *kwela* boys jive down the street
past lush suburban gardens
hoses playing in the heat,
stamping out their rhythms
to the shrill tin whistle
and the hot bass thud,
the tune still insistent
a thread in the distance –

> *A-ma-LE-le, ku-LE-le –*
> *Everyone is singing!*

Black on White

When Anne and I
both born there,
say *South Africa*,
the clipped-off vowels
and crippled consonants
scuttle over
corrugated iron roofs,
barbed wire
and tamped-down drought-hard paths
in barren 'Locations' –
black on white
guilty   fearful
in the glare.

When Margaret,
who's never been there,
says *Africa – ah – Africa*,
the continent stretches sensuously,
muscles ripple beneath its tawny skin.
Big-breasted women rest
in purple shade
and sing.
Then Africa shakes out its mane
of highveld grass
and great striped beasts
lift up their heads
to sniff the rain.

Passionfruit

At night the possums drum the dark
to rage among the tangled vines
of slender, tendrilled passionfruit
and tear the moon down with their sighs.

They rip the tender golden skins,
devour the flesh with cruel mouths,
rampage and riot on the roof
and stutter their impassioned cries.

A dawn wind shreds the clouds and blows
the yellow litter from the vines
across the deck. I wake from dreams
of chill disquiet – to love and loss.

Of things being various

A salute to Louis MacNeice

In the cool blueness of early morning
I carry the washing to the line.
She-oak needles, overlaid with ginger catkins
in hieroglyph patterns, cushion my tread.
Three potoroos, white tail-tips pale in the sun,
hop sedately across my path, disappear into bushland.

On the estuary yachts set sail
for the holiday as my daughter phones
from before-dawn Tianjin: *There's a dust storm
blowing off the Gobi – the wind's rattling the trees.
It's minus sixteen here today.*
Soon, in thermals, face mask and Antarctic jacket,
she'll be fighting a gritty gale to work.
A light breeze has sprung up and the yachts
are moving lazily down river out of sight.

The radio drones its inevitable bad news –
increasing road tolls, mayhem in the Middle East,
a list of extinct species.
                                      I pare six apples
for a pie, steadily circling each sphere
to loosen the green peel, and toss the spirals
on the she-oak carpet. Soon a young wallaby
will appear from beneath the tree ferns
where rosellas strip leaflets from a frond.

Cutting up pumpkin, I breathe the scent
of apples and cloves as the phone rings,
bringing news of an old friend's death.

Shadows move slowly across the table
where I write, marvelling at a world
that is *suddener...and more of it than we think.*

Words Fall as Rain

She wakes one morning
to find words dancing round her head.
No longer marshalled, drilled and rationed,
coldly caged in bureaucratic prose –

>> they're out on the town
>> surging and spinning,
>> scattering meaning,
>> profligate on the page.

In joyful strings they stream across the ceiling,
leap dance out the windows,
festoon the gum trees,
conga across the river
to somersault across the hills
of her horizon.

Some words emerge
with orderly precision
in neat grey suits and pale ties
but they're jostled, trampled
by the riotous throng
tumbling and singing in holiday array.

Ducking and dancing
they skid across the paper,
scattering commas and dashes,
taking the mickey
out of staid semicolons,
making mayhem of meaning.
Romping across black holes
> they split their atoms
>> laughing round the sun.

When the evening music starts
they swing into the great dance,
stream across the stars,
whirl in spiral nebulae,
slide joyously down the great roller coaster
of the Milky Way –

                to fall as rain upon her drought.

Dancing with David Hobson

When David is singing my world turns around –
he holds out his arms and my feet leave the ground.
I'm wearing a dreamy, diaphanous dress
and David's decked out in his svelte evening best –
till I peel off his jacket and loosen his tie,
we kick off our shoes and sing as we fly –

I'm twenty again – lithe, blithe, debonair,
I've left sixty years asleep in the chair –
We dance on the deck lit by headlights of cars,
he holds me so close – I'm sequined with stars.
We glide through the night to 'Impossible Dream',
he sings 'Till There Was You' – oh, what does he mean?

Then I realise he's vanished across the veranda –
but wishing's more sexy than full-frontal candour!

suddenly spring…

bubbles through bitumen
leapfrogs fences
trumpets
this glory morning
on sassy saxophones
silver-dazzle showers
larrup the dust
scattering winter

hot pink
winds
whirl
plastic wrappers
flick skirts
flash
knickers
kick
tin cans
tinkling
among alley cats
leaping
at butterflies
in the spring-dingle sunshine
of this zip-tooting
morning

Your skin to my touch...

fine silk
worn vellum.
Fingering the stops of your spine
I improvise the music of our lives
listen to your body's counterpoint
soft breath   heart's pulse
old discords
moving toward
peaceful resolution.

The gourd of your head
rests close to my own
your shoulder girdle
moves gently beneath my hands –
softness of belly
hardness of thighs.

We rest in interior darkness
warm   at peace
and for a moment
shut out the knowledge
that this little death
prefigures one to come
when the swallow spirit
will fly from the bone house.

In the morning –
breakfasting in sunshine
gold of marmalade
yeastiness of toast –
we revel in the moment
as rosellas
splash rainbows
in the birdbath.

I peel an orange
oil from the skin
pungent on my hands.

Talk

Take my hand
come with me downstairs,
unlock the cellar door,
pull out the boxes,
open up the trunks,
let out the ghosts,
let in the sunlight.

Or will we continue
to deny the dark tides,
dam them up behind
polite facades, acquiescent nods,
mild words and tiny smiles,
till the hurricane
tears the words from our teeth,
the rising flood
sweeps out the rotting boxes
as the ark
sails past
without us?

Come, take my hand.

On Peron Dunes

After days of wild seas
the wind has dropped, the dunes
swept bare. I walk the shadowed valleys
to the shore, awed by destruction's beauty.

Turning to search the sky
for resident sea eagles,
I see instead, contoured on a sandhill's crest,
two young lovers, naked bodies gilded
by the sun's last rays.

I look away
but my eye has caught the image,
the ardour of their wild coupling.
She arches up to meet his body
curved above her in pulsating air,
her hair a glittering cascade, the dune
thrusting them toward the sky.

Late light glances off the boomer crests.
Pacific gulls pick over piles of storm wrack.
Then, above the shouting surf,
I hear the clamour of sea eagles,
watch them circle westward,
soaring in their courtship dance –
until I'm dazzled by the setting sun.

Siren Song

At daybreak they tumbled into the bay
where I swam, gliding past me
through the silk-green roll of the tide,
black fins tracking their path back to sea.
I heard her singing, the girl on the beach,
singing in the sea wind as I drifted
in the lift of the tide.
                Under the she-oaks
at sunset she sang and they came again
glinting through the darkening water,
arc after black arc leaping,
dripping gold in the last light.
All night I drifted with the dolphins –
                sea wind and singing and the sea
                in my body, moored to the moon.

saltwater dreams

underwater
on the edge of no-breath
I dive down
to a time before no-time
when my cells floated free
oscillated in warm seas

as whales plunge
and spout
across the horizon
sounding
their ancient songs
I taste the salty moment
when hair and nails
were protective scales
feet and fingers
fused to flippers

emerging at the edge of the Bight
evolving from fish to mammal
I graze on succulent leaves
and in a flash of recognition
beyond imagination
know them to give life

Adrift in the Desert

for Helen Mills

The wind sweeps in under the rim of day,
builds miniature sand dunes, obliterates
the tracks of yesterday.
Gathering random botanical names
that litter the desert we crouch
beside a sprawling plant – microscopic
flowers hide beneath grey stems
that cling to red sand, each grain a boulder.
Ants harvest seeds, lizards flicker in the stony glitter.
On this calm plain a lifespan
is less than an eye-blink in the millennia
that have passed beneath the relentless sun.

Adrift in the flow of days
we travel toward sunset with no end in sight,
but to float in this moment.
Tonight will fold stars about us,
tomorrow will arrive to a fanfare of magpies.

Cook

After 'Adlestrop' by Edward Thomas

Yes, I remember Cook – the train
stopped there one hot September morning.
No platform – just the hard red earth.
We scrambled down to stretch our legs

surprised to find four flowering gums
where waves of bluebush lapped the plain.
A goods train lurched across our view
dragging interminable clanking trucks,

at last contracting to a smudge
at the eastern rim of an ancient sea.
Then in the stillness a bird churred
harshly from the eucalypts –

and all the honeyeaters of the Nullarbor
came shrieking and shrilling, smothering
the blossom, rollicking in redness
while the trees shook their leaves –
                    or clapped their hands –

and the bluebush plain flowed on and on
under a shimmering sky.

Purnululu Pilgrimage

In midday heat
a line of ant-like figures
threads its way through
Piccaninny Gorge.
Past sandstone cliffs
striped black with lichen
we disappear into a vaulted sepulchre.
From a hole high overhead
light streams to a pool
where the pale leaf-moon
lies drowned amid unfathomable skies.
The pilgrims move into the darkness
footfall silent on the sand.

Wandjina figures tower about us
shifting shadows flicker   fade.
Our guide, transformed to priestess,
lifts a cooling melon from the pool,
carves and carries it to each in turn –
we nod our silent thanks.

Clothed in mystery
we stumble back to our own time
as a tourist chopper stutters overhead.

At midnight,
awed to silence,
we listen to the colloquy of frogs,
howling dingoes, barking owls –
trace the pathway of a satellite
beneath a shower of stars.

Ruined Piano Sanctuary

Released
from suburban drawing rooms,
bead curtains, oils of highland cattle,
a piano glimmers in the moonlit bush.
A dawdling heifer materialises
through early morning mist,
gently licks the feltless hammers.

No longer bound
by sonatinas, pale fingers,
or polite applause,
it disintegrates
in the slow days
amid long grass and ghostly gums.

At moonrise
wind shreds the veneer,
mice scrabble up the backboard,
plink across the keyboard.

The farm cat takes its nightly walk.

*

In the swamp
a legless pub piano
slumps against a tree,
gum leaves fill the keyboard spaces,
discarded ivories
glint beneath the water –
tadpoles
like grace notes
skitter downstream.

*

An old grand rests rakishly
on a rise between the rocks.
One leg lost, lid raised defiantly –
it waits through the long nights
for the maestro to appear.

Wind hums through the wires
drones through the bass notes
whispers fragments of Satie.

*

In the shallows
half-hidden by the rushes
like Moses-in-a-basket,
a bleached and bow-legged piano
from an outback farmstead
sucks up water, slackens,
dreams of the spinster lady
who brought it by camel
to her brother's farm.

Nightly
starlight flickers on brass pedals
that remember her tiny slippers,
the tentative touch
of her long skirts,
the singing classes
she conducted
for the station children.

Now green tree frogs
swarm beneath the backboard,
frolic on the strings,
transform it
to a wild hurdy-gurdy.

*

Beside a windmill
turning slowly in the heat –
clack plunk-er-plunk –
lie fragments of a candelabra,
a warped keyboard
and music stand
scattered in the bracken.

At dusk
a kangaroo probes
the wreckage with its delicate nose,
licks the moonlight off the keys.

Assisi

for Joan Tiller

At our *pensione* window
in a modest convent
you sit to draw an early plum in bloom.
Over your bent head
I watch the doves and ravens
feeding peacefully
below the olive trees.

In spring sunshine
an old man reads a newspaper,
covers his knees
with rumours of a war.
A sudden gust
silvers the olives.

A white cat steps sedately
across faded terracotta tiles,
drops on its belly to stalk
a lizard basking in the sun.

Ravens circle the tower
as slow bells sound
across the smoky Umbrian plain.
Shadows elongate and paint the walls.

Slowly you put your pencil down
to look – and look.

*

We walk the pilgrim's way up to the Hermitage
past olive groves where children gather prunings
for Palm Sunday Mass – an ancient nun,
dark raven flapping in the breeze,
calls them to her side.
We stop to eat our lunch –
bread and crumbly cheese,
olives, two blood oranges.
Sitting on a pile of olive cuttings,
cushioned on the gritty shale,
we squeeze a small libation to the saint.

We climb the path as you recite
the unfamiliar canticle of northern spring:
> charlock and aconite,
> monk's hood or wolf-bane,
> a small gleam of violets,
> daisies, grape-hyacinths,
> blackthorn in early bud,
> glistening celandines,
> a clump of primroses.

In the deeply shaded garden
at the Hermitage
school children, scattering noise and litter,
scramble from grumbling buses.
White doves fuss and croodle on the grass
below a statue of the saint,
his hands outstretched,
a perch for plaster birds.
A stone wall hides a dried-up stream
choked with dead leaves, mud
and scurrying grey shadows.

*

Standing at the Rocca
in the wind we turn to see
the hills patched bronze –
winter beech woods
veined with snow.

At our feet a crocus, purple-blue,
pushes through the grass,
iridescent flies cling to clumps
of glossy angelica,
golden wallflowers bloom
in crevices of broken stone.

Slowly we descend the steps
past gardens sheltering
behind locked gates.
Out of the wind early forsythia is still.
An old dog sleeps in a warm corner,
opens an eye as we pass
and sleeps again.

*

At her Basilica we view Saint Clare,
dug up a century ago, now on display
decked out in a stiff new habit –
a wimple round her mottled skull
and rosary in skeletal hands –
she's laid out under glass, grinning darkly,
and set about with tawdry gifts and candles.
Challenged by the face of death,
we retreat into the fading light
where children play a counting game,
their voices fly between the deep-toned bells
that toll the evening office.

Round the corner youths on mopeds,
girls on pillions, putt-putt past us
shouting cheerful insults to the children.

*

After supper at the convent,
packing to move on next day,
we contemplate the irony
of Clare being patron saint of television.
Poor Clare, who had eschewed
all wealth and all possessions,
had in her last illness,
so her followers declared,
seen and heard the Mass
upon the bare walls of her cell.

From our window
we watch grinning ravens
swarm round the tower
to settle for the night.

Leaving Beijing – Terminal 3

In this enormous aviary of glass and steel
we float through airy spaces
winging our way to the top floor
for a farewell lunch.
Sipping pale chrysanthemum tea,
we share salads of shredded papaya,
pomelo and prawns –
all delicate crunch, cool succulence,
memories of surf and orchards wet with dew.

Ghost-like, across the plain,
Beijing, the fashionable Phoenix
rising from Imperial ashes,
glimmers through a pall of smog.

Last words and promises and hugs.

Once through Departure I look back to wave
and see your tears – the unrelenting separation begins.
The escalator glides toward the skytrain
that whisks its load along the dragon's tail.
At the tip, I board my plane back to Audahlia –
as I've learned to speak of home.

The dragon's breath fogs the window.
I view cold milky coffee, insipid pasta
untouched on my supper tray –
the taste of pomelo and prawns still lively in my mouth,
the saltiness of separation.

Digging

for Alice

Digging in her sandpit,
shell grit and river sand,
I unearth another sandpit where a child
wearing nothing but a hat
feeds sand and water to a patient dog,
Come Bob, eat your porridge.
He sneaks behind the house
to spit it out.

Dig deeper to a Cape Town garden
where my mother ties a bonnet
on her cat, sings it to sleep
beneath her father's flapping shirts.

Dig down to a London park
where a small girl wheels
her brother's pram beside the pond,
sees her reflection dissolve
into her mother chasing chickens
from a Dorset kitchen,
then into her grandmother cutting
peat in County Clare.

Dig back to generations of small girls
who gather fleece from brambles,
twirl spindles, wind wool,
cup eggs in careful hands,
teach the toddler, hush the baby,
draw their names on sandy floors.

Today we're building castles in her sandpit.
My granddaughter's warm hands
draw gritty patterns on my cheek.
She takes the spade
               — *It's my turn now.*

Grandmother Annie

Out of the strong came forth sweetness... Judges 14:14

Apple-cheeked Annie, from the banks
of the Derbyshire Derwent, sailed to the Cape
to marry her childhood sweetheart, Harry,
railwayman, brass foundry worker,
forging links with a new country.

Straight away he began tempering her
to the rule of his exacting God.
Nine months later she bore a son
and almost died delivering
his thirteen vigorous pounds.

*

One winter night, while Father
held forth at a temperance meeting,
gentle Annie and her son played cards,
enjoying an evening's respite
from the keeper of the law.

A childish game of Snap it was
but retribution waited in the dark.
Father returned, denounced the devil
and his playthings, cast the cards
into the fiery furnace.

*

On Fridays she would rise at five
to roll her pastry on the marble slab
and through the pantry window see,
past the blue plumbago hedge and far
across the veld, cool hills of home
and imagine she smelled rain.

Turning, she'd lift the pastry tenderly
to make her legendary pies,
and stoke the fires of persevering love
to bake her kisses and her 'come-love' cakes.
By then the righteous deity
had begun to melt a little.

That was a century ago and now
she slips into my daughter's kitchen
to roll her pastry, stir her cakes
and through the window sees
an antipodean Derwent,
a world away from home.

Poem Rising

At dusk stirring the soup
I hear the first faint plop,
                    see a quick edge of light,
glinting sounds – then gone.
After tea I'll land this one
before it plunges to the bottom.

Scramble through the washing-up,
fish the last teaspoon
from the iridescent bubbles,
wipe my hands –
       Now!
                The phone rings
and I tune out as she tells me
of her recent haul.
Inside, I'm listening to the poem rising.
       Now, here's a line –
             I hang up.
Too late – it's off the hook.
I try to lure it to the surface
but the pool's opaque
muddied by effort and frustration.

Tired to bed
to dream of dark pools,
shadowy shapes beneath the water,
frail sounds that break
in circles of light.

In the morning I'll dredge the darkness,
gently tickle it to the surface,
knowing that its sheen will fade
in the plain light of day –
when I'll have to take and make phone calls
        wash dishes
               make soup –
                      plop!

Wool Gathering

Grandma farmed the Scottish highlands
while Grandpa hunted grouse. She herded
her children – the youngest to glean fleece
from gorse bushes, the boys to shear
her stubborn sheep, the girls to card
and spin long staples – while she roamed
the glens collecting plants to dye the yarn
in cauldrons, to an heirloom recipe.

On winter nights, young 'uns abed,
her eldest daughter helped her warp
the loom to weave the old twill patterns
of heather, mist and gorse,
her tongue clack-clacking
to the rhythm as she told
the peat-dark highland yarns.
She wove eight rugs – one for each child.

My mother's rug was underfoot
in wedding photos, a carpet for white silk.
It tagged along on her honeymoon,
a familiar island on foreign beaches,
the magic carpet that brought them to Tasmania,
my brother's comfort blanket until the dogs
claimed it on the sleep-out bed –
the remnants lined a basket for the cat.

Now Grandma's in a Weaver's Paradise
where sheep are rainbow-coloured
and fleece is free for all to gather.
She floats above the paddocks
in the gossamer shroud she spun and felted
in her eighties. Just below the clouds
she drops it on the river, to dissolve
in filaments of winter mist.

Lucy Turns the World

Morning by morning   she left by the front door
weighed down with tools   walked down the hill
tarred paths frosted   water gurgling in gutters
came to the field   barren with rain
through years of winter   to dig out stones
hard ringing on iron   sharp piercing shards
buried long years back   piled up stones
for holding in   for keeping out
for marking boundaries.   Thoughts of walls
made the stone heap grow.

This morning they go   out through the back door
tools forgotten   she and the child
push through banksias   brimming with birds
choose the pathway   past the grevilleas.
The child picks a grass stem   to fathom the puddles
shakes the acacias   sodden with rain
scatters rosellas   and climbs up the stone heap:
I'm on top of the mountain   the sun's in a puddle
I hold out my arms   the sky flies around me
I can turn the whole world.

Boy on the Trampoline

Out early this winter morning
he bounces over the low red sun,
a dark bird or descending angel,
wings spread wide against the pale sky.
Folding himself neatly he somersaults
into adolescence.

Life is tough, learn to roll with the punches.
Trouble is coming, sorrow is coming –
but that's not the whole story –
so leap into life, Ben, spring into joy.

For the tear is an intellectual thing
(William Blake)

Guided by his father's arm
the boy lurches to his seat
in the front row.
The curtain rises
on tribal dancers whirling
round the fire. Their world, invaded,
begins to change forever.
A young girl is abducted
from her plundered people
to become the toy of her protectors.

The boy in the front row begins to wail –
softly at first, turns his head
from side to side in unspeakable pain.
His father cannot comfort him
and leads him from the theatre.

His desolate keening fades
but it has entered the dance,
has become one with the bird cries,
the chanting, the clicking sticks.
Mathinna in her red dress
is abandoned, raped,
her people left derelict and dying.

His cries live inside us,
his tears on our cheeks.

Mathinna: a girl's journey between two cultures was performed in the Theatre Royal, Hobart, by the Bangarra Dance Theatre, with Elma Kris as Mathinna, at the end of October 2010.

Wybelena Moonbirds

The wind, the wind blows
all night through the she-oaks,
shadows merge and flicker
over emptied graves.

Dark figures carry the remains
of grandmothers long gone,
lithe girls who slithered over rocks
to hunt for seals.

Wrapped in bark and twine
the precious bundles are ferried silently
to unmarked graves
on nameless islands.

The wind, the wind keens,
silvering the flattened trefoil
planted on the emptied graves
to deceive the body-hunters.

Before dawn
moonbirds lift into the wind,
eerie cries
silenced by the restless strait.

She-oak at First light

Allocasuarina monolifera

Red filament-flowers
threaded with diamonds of frost
festoon your sprawling branches.

A flock of firetails alight,
nuzzle your ruby stamens,
flaunt red bottoms, tilt in the wind.

Fluffed-up fledglings bounce
along your slender stems,
nibble your sparkling necklace.

A grey fantail dances on air,
swooping arabesques
looping your silvery spangles.

The golden whistler flings
his saucy song across the garden
as the sun beats its gong
over the fog-filled valley.

Old Men and Birds

Tianjin, March 2008

Plodding through the *hutongs*, old men
swing covered cages, pick their way
round building sites where China
reinvents herself. Frosty puddles
mirror the smog of early morning.
Muffled against the seeping cold
they gather in the open space above the metro –
mutilated shrubs make this a park –
and stand their cages on the sparse grey grass.
Covers lifted, the mynahs start to sing.
One man scoops his bird from the cage,
slips a silk noose round its neck
and strokes it gently. Ecstatic
at his tender touch, the bird
throws back its head to sing
the sweetest, saddest song – the men
crowd closer, drawn by some ancient alchemy
they cannot name.

From the Drum Tower that afternoon an old man
sets a flock of pigeons free, watches as they wheel
and turn as one, a silver, indigo, then violet cloud,
swooping and climbing in the dying light.
He holds out grain-filled hands
and lures them back into captivity.

From the far country of grief they come…

in the early light of dawn
hollow with loss and clothed in unfamiliar beauty.

Through the flickering mirage they stumble toward us
bearing – oh, so tenderly – their terrible load.

We reach out to embrace them
but they are the untouchables who have fed on bitter bread.

We speak to them across the chasm
but our words fall at our feet.

They listen for a language we have not learned,
see the lost one in turned heads,
a figure disappearing in the crowd.

On the cliffs they pause
to stare at shapes that gather
in the fog drift of the sea…

the restless sea,
endlessly singing
is now and ever shall be.

Raymond

I remember your quiff of fair hair lifted by the wind,
your sharp boy-sweat smell when we climbed trees,
the way your thumb straightened when you held the bat.
I remember, as we walked beneath the willows,
your gentle touch on the back of my hand,
your voice saying, in your mysterious mother-tongue,
Je t'aime – did you know I understood?

I remember your birthday picnic, the ambrosial cake
your mother sent from the farm, the thirteen white candles
blown out by the breeze before you could make a wish.
I remember the click-click-click of wheels
as we pushed our bikes uphill that last afternoon.

I remember the long night of the accident,
        the blank days that followed,
                the silence.

Letter to Peggy

i.m. Peggy Coombs

Today we visited your garden
beside the bay at Esterbrook –
the sands pale apricot and ochre
ribbed and marbled by the tides.
Sky and water, border salvias
blue as borage, where the bees
crawl on clover, seeding parsley,
hum round runner-beans, sweet peas.

Fruiting vines festoon the windows
filtering sunlight through the rooms.
Beneath the glass the grapes are ripening
rich golden brown, one spray of leaves
already seared and veined with purple,
mulberry, plum, flavescent, blue,
like your wools still in the basket,
from fleeces you and David grew.

First day of autumn – David's birthday,
friends are leaving after lunch,
goodbyes beside the bright geraniums –
…*the garden's just as she had planned…*
we pause to touch the fading roses,
fragrance rising in the heat.

Now the Chinese elms you planted
shade the empty garden seat.

Woman in the Jade Felt Hat

In her jade felt hat
she sits at the entrance to the gallery,
a rough wooden cross at her throat,
her face as youthful, as beautiful
as when we met years ago.
An heirloom seal-fur coat conceals
shards of a shattered life:
eccentric parents, bursts of schizophrenia,
an alcoholic marriage, a feckless son.
Friendless, she's washed up on this foreign shore.

Like my cross? I carved it in the prison camp.
Looks good, don't you think?
I see no one now.
I'm a shut-in, but stirred myself today,
despite the weather, to see the exhibition.

The paintings pale beside the portrait
at the entrance to the gallery:
Woman in the Jade Felt Hat.

When you phoned last night...

your voice
danced like prayer flags on a mountain,
glinted and sang
like rapids over greenstone.

Your pain and weakness forgotten
together we crested sand dunes,
splashed through waves,
and swam towards the sun.

What do you see as you
look over the rim of the world?

What fills you with such delight?
For a moment,
we both forgot
the imminent full stop.

Letter to Jean

i.m. Jean Young

Today I made a chocolate cake
from the recipe you gave me.
I hoped you'd come, a welcome visitant,
but not a sign
until the mixture dimpled in the bowl.
Had you stuck a finger in
to test consistency?

I try to be consistent
but gave up the day I missed a visit
and never got to say goodbye.

When you were dying
I stood outside your house
in late winter sunshine
marvelling at leaves and buds
unfolding on dry sticks,
a quince hedge stirring to new life.

Now we've eaten the cake
and bottled the quinces.

Another summer draws to a close.

The tempest in my mind

i.m. Joe Claessens

Adrift
in a storm-ravaged ship,
rudder broken,

ropes unravelling,
maps dissolving,
bleeding their colours

across damp clouds,
he comes at length to a shore
familiar yet strange.

Tides have obliterated
print, word, image
as, broken compass in hand,

he leans uncertainly into the wind
…the tempest in my mind…
and for a breath

knows what he has lost.
Salt on his cheeks, he stumbles
as the tide turns

erasing every footprint.
The beach lies
blank again.

*

He has always carried keys
cold metal
in slippery sweaty fingers,

useless now.
Shapes slither, twist and bend.
Dali knew it all.

Nothing fits.
He wanders
from parent to parent

wife to child,
son of a strong mother
and faithless father,

inhabiting each
for a shadowy moment.
Face pressed to the glass

slowly he falls sideways
groping for the handle
of a door that is forever locked.

*

Through the glass
he sees the magnolia
in tight green bud

tokens of
meaningless spring
meaningless

as the flowers his daughter
sent for his wife's birthday.
Flocks of hands

fly up
to touch him gently
help him shower

dress and eat.
And he wonders why
she never comes

yet knows these hands are hers.
He fumbles for an image
that eludes him,

the young girl he bought flowers for
in Cape Town.
A butterfly settles on a leaf.

*

Snow in November
swirling across spring suburbs
brutal, untimely.

Cloud shadows
race across the mountain.
The wind bites chill

as he walks – walks endlessly
through doorways,
along garden paths,

lost in a maze
of chaotic fragments –
Don't talk – just walk

he mutters and clasps her hand
as they pass ordered flower beds
boronia, daisies, lavender.

A trail of roses
tugs at his memory.
Disfigured – utterly disfigured

he mourns, shuffling
through drifts of apple blossom.
Look, snow on the mountain.

He stumbles on
seeing only the whirling blizzard
that whites out his world.

The Unravelling

Three children, a dingy
and a sudden storm

two swim ashore
the girl is trapped below

                     wind and water
                     unravelling   unravelling

after the funeral
her father fills the dingy
with her ashes, dancing shoes and teddy bear

sets them ablaze
turns the boat into the current

                     wind and water
                     unravelling   unravelling

her mother, grief-hollowed,
kneels on the stones
her brothers, bewildered   stand   apart

her father stares down
at his blackened hands

                     wind and water   wind and water
                     unravelling   unravelling.

Onions and Aftershave

She says she's over it
can even talk about it
when she has to
but standing in the kitchen
peeling onions
first the crackly russet skin
then the next layer
>staring out at the trees
>glistening in the rain
>not seeing them   not seeing
>the burnt purple scars
>on the trunks
she peels off another layer.
The centre's all that's left
its pearly whiteness
slimy grey.
She drops it in the bin.

One day she may be able
to smell the rain
damp earth and tangy eucalypt

now all she can smell
onions
– and aftershave.

Coffee at the Signal Station Café

28 April 2011

Autumn stillness,
a warm blue day
with just an edge of winter.
Below us brown islands sprawl
in the quiet estuary.
The Iron Pot points an accusing finger
at a band of dark pollution
drifting south.

At a nearby table
old friends are catching up –
speak of their work,
of mutual friends. She tells
of plans for her daughter,
shows photographs –
scraps of conversation
drift across the coffee.

I was there, he says, *at Port Arthur…*
but in the morning, before it happened…
…fifteen years ago today…
we were at school together, he and I,
…we always kept in touch…
he lost them all…his whole family…
…those two small girls…
She reaches out to touch his arm.
His silence reaches out to us.

On sloping lawns autumnal shrubs
flaunt red leaves about to fall.
We look across calm waters
to the Tasman hills
as time collapses –
no longer holding days apart.

Every Day a Blue Door

A blue door creaks,
clings by a single hinge,
just a door
swinging in the after-shock,
splintered wood   beaten earth   mangled tin.

As Szymborska said – *after every war*
someone has to clean up –
bring in sniffer dogs, bulldozers,
scrape up remains, defuse landmines.

But for now,
a blue door
opening onto empty sky –
that is if you choose not to look down,
choose not to see,
protruding from the rubble,
a small arm.

> Warlords and politicians
> retreat to the capital,
> consign language
> to collateral damage.

You could rewind,
redesign the scene,
add gardens, huts,
high-rises – or fast-forward
a couple of centuries to triumphant
archaeologists unearthing remnants
of a blue door.

But for now,
just the agonised creaking
and a small arm,
not waving.

Every Twenty-two Minutes

Red lilies lie dormant
across rice paddies and hillsides,
bulbs buried near schools and temples
ready to burst into flower.
They need careful handling, these red lilies,
gross feeders on blood and bone.

In villages, in fields, on jungle paths
children dig for iron to sell as scrap,
cuddle bomblets,
toy with landmines
on the edge of craters,
dream of feeding their families,
weigh the future in small hands.

In a moment
maimed and broken
they mutate
to ephemeral lilies
that explode and die.

In complacent countries
grown fat from investments in armaments
we donate crutches and prostheses –

and plant more seeds
to ensure a constant crop of red lilies.

The Wasteland – Ninety Years on

October
        is the fractured month/moth, brooding wingless
            in the corneal city, toppling, barren,
                into no-spring, no-lilacs,
                      sheep no longer safely graze.

At the cracked centre below the oceans,
            death spawns
under the yellow eye of Midas,
            black gold spits its poisons into the sea.

        Plastics disintegrate to pseudo-plankton,
        fill the bellies of albatross chicks in death rookeries.
        Acid oceans leach the skeletons of micro-organisms,
        currents alter course, El Niño distends to gargantua.

Where are the philosophers, the theists, the atheists?

Detritus fouls beaches,
tar balls, *hush, oh my tarbaby*. Wetlands burn, blacken,
light thickens, hubris
stalks boardrooms and parliaments.

        Cracks appear beneath the surface of violent cities,
        tremors/volcanoes. Power-brokers spout
        unctuous promises, dismiss maternal lamentations,
        ignore the blinded hordes/herds.

Babel lies in ruins. Turn on your multi-channel TV,
increase the volume. From dry wells, from iphones,
voices whisper globalese,
      drown out faint cries
           of *shantih*   *shantih*
              peace to you, blue planet.

Flying West

Leaving the island
sculpted by Antarctic winds,
riven by channels and moody inlets,
we fly above folded farmlands,
humped hills concealed
in wombat vegetation.
As we cross the wrinkled strait
the island shrinks beneath a continent of cloud.

Flying west
we cross the parched interior
pursued by the plane's moth image.
A flotsam of dark scrub
transforms to mythic figures
that stalk the ancient seabed
where time long since ran dry.

Landfall in the west –
extravagant sandscapes,
elongated ranges,
wrinkles ironed out.
Days expand along wide beaches.
We swim beyond the breakers,
look back to see the city's skyline
sprawl to the escarpment.

Heat, honey-thick and golden,
slicks our bodies,
the dazzle-disk horizon
spins about us.
Night's extravaganza begins
as fireball Sol dives
sizzling into the ocean,
and the Seven Sisters
tilt singing
toward the Cross.

Artists Retreat from Jeanneret Beach

Artists have ambushed the bay,
Jeanneret Beach is under siege.
They hide under she-oaks, in shadows of rocks,
      erect their easels in marram grass
            beneath black and green umbrellas,
lash their coats about them, train their gaze on –
      a composition.

The sea battens down
      behind the rocks,
           behind the headland, behind the dunes –
even the kelp lies doggo in the shallows.
The horizon has ruled out variations,
      individual interpretations
           and darkens unfathomably
as a ship slips over the line.

Some attack the bay head-on, hoping
to snatch a seascape/rockscape/landscape
while maintaining perspective, scale and tonal unity.
The wind brings up cloud reinforcements
but the invaders see the sky as a wash,
      an expanse controlling the painting
           controlled by the artist
or, like Fred Williams, don't bother with sky at all.

Late afternoon, they retreat from the chilling breeze.
The bay is released from their stern surveillance,
      personal perspectives, reductions to scale.

Gulls settle on the beach.
Kelp uncoils in the seething tide.
As the sea reappears from behind rocks, headland, dunes,
the sky, high as a kite, escapes from the frame
      and disappears into the blue.

Pointed Bone

Suspended rib
hip bone
single vertebra
pterodactyl beak
whispers
above the hesitations
above the gaps and glances.
Bare bone
mouthing emptiness.
What was hidden is now exposed.
Just give it a pair of eyes and toenails
and it will perform
the poem for us.

Hearing it dance
tapping to the tune
of the tendons snapping,
rapping out a rhythm
on the splintered bone,
I keep my head down
pencil point on paper
waiting for the dancer's
final incarnation.

The Galaxies of Jackson Pollock

for Joan Tiller

At the Pompidou we rode the space-age lifts
hoping to find art – not industry – concealed
behind the modernist façade of coloured steel.
Amused by Man Ray's tongue-in-cheekiness,
his peachy bottoms and punning installations,
we turned aside to view
the Jackson Pollock retrospective.
Recalling the press panning of *Blue Poles,*
I'd come to mock – but stood transfixed…

Next day we wandered through Montmartre.
At *Sonja et Carlos* we feasted on sole *Meurnière*,
asparagus and brie. In a haze of house rosé,
we shrugged aside a visit to the Louvre,
returned instead to the embrace
of Pollock's fields of light,
whirling us out to galaxies
where colours yet to be conceived
await their birth.

Dancing with the Sun

a salute to John Olsen

Celebrating eighty-five years
in this *mud-puddle-wonderful* world
he stands in orange socks and green jumper
at the centre of an enormous canvas,
Where there's white, there's hope, he laughs,
sweeping his brush in a sun-circle.

His helper holds him by one hand
as they dance a slow sock-sarabande
back and forth across the canvas.
Wielding the long-handled brush
he twists and curves the paint-tracks,
I'm taking a line for a walk.

Exuberantly he bangs his brush,
splashes paint with incandescent joy,
The soul must sing!
He adds a dash of red,
a final flourish of jumper-green –
the king-sun appears, blazing life and energy –

    Hello, Sun!

www.ingramcontent.com/pod-product-compliance
Lightning Source LLC
Chambersburg PA
CBHW070050120526
44589CB00034B/1731